Ultimate Reality

You Can't Get There from Here …

SEAN M. WILLETT

WESTBOW
PRESS®
A DIVISION OF THOMAS NELSON
& ZONDERVAN

WestBow Press books may be ordered through booksellers or by contacting:

WestBow Press
A Division of Thomas Nelson & Zondervan
1663 Liberty Drive
Bloomington, IN 47403
www.westbowpress.com
1 (866) 928-1240

ISBN: 978-1-9736-2045-7 (sc)
ISBN: 978-1-9736-2046-4 (e)

Library of Congress Control Number: 2018903189

Print information available on the last page.

WestBow Press rev. date: 04/02/2018

"You can't get there from here." The irony of that statement is highly subjective. It's obvious to most that those words, spoken by so many, offer a bit of confusion to the listener as the mind downshifts from analytical mode to a full memory scan in a fraction of a second. While pondering this notion, you can only come to one logical conclusion: the person who spoke those words only knows how to get to the destination in question from another location that he or she is familiar with. Most of us think in terms of relativity—people, places or things we have experienced or to which we have some point of reference.

I have often found myself thinking those same comical words in frustration while trying to convince another of my perspective. There have been many times when I've tried to share with others, in truth, concepts that I strongly believe in, only to walk away feeling unsuccessful. My wife and I have endeavored to raise five children into adulthood—a not-so-easy task when viewed in contrast to all the other innate concerns and troubles of everyday life. It is highly frustrating to want so greatly to lead someone that you love so much in what you know is the right direction for his or her life, only to find that your efforts have been at best fruitless. It is heartbreaking to watch those you love suffer from poor decisions that have been made in the past, especially those you have made. I find it difficult, to say the least, to know how to communicate affirming words of love to those who plainly don't want them. Expressing your concerns for their safety, wellbeing, and ultimately happiness can often prove to be quite a challenge while trying to process all those mixed emotions that never seem to untangle. I find myself thinking, *If I could only somehow impart to them the knowledge and experience I have obtained in my life through learning from the school of hard knocks without them knowing that it was me trying to convince them of these truths. They would probably latch on and take it to heart.* Of course, I suppose that would rob them of the whole learning experience. I remember many times in my life when I was perplexed and overwhelmed and just needed answers. After flipping through the pages of the Bible for a while, staggering through the thees and thous in search for substantial truth to change my situation, I would toss it back on the bookshelf. You could almost see the word *frustrated* forming in the thin cloud of dust rolling off the shelf. The intended theme of this letter largely coincides with a story I heard on the radio once; consider the following a paraphrase.

> One Sunday morning a farmer was reading a book in the comfort of his warm home during a frigid winter storm. He was distracted by the sound of irregular rapping at the kitchen door. The distraction was caused by young birds that were disoriented by the storm flying repeatedly into the storm door that led into the kitchen. Moved with compassion, he propped the door open, endeavoring to lead the young ones to safety from the storm. They immediately flew away to a small tree near the barn. Unwilling to give up, he prepared himself and left the comfort of his home and continued in his attempt to rescue the young birds. He opened the large barn door for them, yet the birds would not enter the barn. He began shaking the tree, but still they would not go. He threw some straw in the air to lead them into flight in hopes that they would enter the barn, yet still they would not go. Exhausted in frustration, he hopelessly stood there thinking, *If I could only become a bird, then they would trust me enough to follow me into the safety of the barn.* He must have been thinking, *You just can't get there from here.* When he heard the sounds of the church bells off in the distance, a look of astonishment consumed his face as he realized that must have been how the Lord felt before He left the comfort of His heavenly home to come here and show His people the way to the safety and security of His salvation.

I've found that trying to convince anyone of anything without first considering his or her point of view on the subject is often futile. It seems to me that to successfully communicate an idea or notion to another, it is almost always necessary to leave your perspective and as much as possible, identify with the other individual or group of individuals on a personal level. Put yourself in their shoes, and try to see life through their eyes from their set of circumstances—or make the effort to feel what they feel. I believe in the medical field, they refer to this as transference. Although many times there is the inherent risk of misplaced priority involved with attempting to leave one's own perspective to see another's, I still believe that many times it's the most effective way to communicate. I often wonder that if I would have adapted to that philosophy a little more with my own children, instead of self-righteously laying down the law, perhaps I would have been a little more successful at raising young adults. While the law is necessary in that it creates form and structure, it isn't always very easy to accept when it conflicts with what we think we want.

The Line

GOD HAS WELL ESTABLISHED His laws for us in love and for our benefit, collective and individual, and when we abide by them, we will reap the benefits of obedience. Though they seem abrasive and rigid at times, as they ought, the purpose behind them is ultimately for His glory and subsequently our good. God ordained His laws for us in His divine holy wisdom without consulting us, just as when He created us, in His own image; they're not up for negotiation or debate. The Word of God (Jesus) describes Himself (Jesus)/itself (the Bible) as being limitless and unbiased.

> For the word of God is quick, and powerful, and sharper
> than any two-edged sword, piercing even to the dividing
> asunder of soul and spirit, and of the joints and marrow,
> and is a discerner of the thoughts and intents of the heart.
> (Hebrews 4:12 KJV)

Sharper means being able to cut even to the dividing asunder of soul and spirit, clearly transcending the known physical properties of this world. Double-edged means it will cut in either direction that which is in violation of God's "perfect" will—whether it be the one wielding the sword (speaking the word) or the one the sword is being wielded at (the hearer). As I read once in a very clever analogy, one can disagree with the man-made rules of working with electricity that were designed for the safety of the people that work with, on, or around electrically charged circuits; but that does not negate the intrinsic laws inherent to electricity.

Those laws, when violated, will continue to exist without respect of persons or regard for personal safety or consequence and will do so with raw efficiency. One important characteristic regarding electricity is that you don't necessarily have to physically violate the rule by actually touching the live wire. Under the right circumstances, you need only to be close enough for the electricity to arc or jump to the path of least resistance to ground, which in that case would be you. It behooves us Christians to bear this reality in mind when toying with that upper limit as the word of God is a discerner of the thoughts and intents of the heart. I have a childhood friend who, as a child, endured a very traumatic experience regarding an inadvertent violation of one of those physical laws regarding electricity. In their innocent search for childhood fun, Brian and his younger brother, Mike, substituted a thin spool of wire in the absence of string to playfully fly their kite. Tragically, their kite became entangled in the power lines near the road, and they both have very large scars on their bodies from the surge of electricity that literally blew through their flesh, maintaining strict conformance to the law. Interestingly, Brian later studied to become an electrician in his adult life. Without morbid regurgitation, suffice it to say that many have lost life and others have suffered great injury even to the loss of limbs resulting from not following the uncompromising laws of electricity. Those laws are the result of the trials and errors of many generations of learned truths in the field of electrical engineering based on the physical properties of electricity. How much more pertinent would universal truths designed by an all-knowing, all-seeing, omnipresent God be? Bear in mind that in the times of the Old Testament humans were under the active wrath of God, and since the crucifixion, burial, and resurrection of Christ, humanity is now under the passive wrath of God as we are now in the age of grace. In an Old Testament account, Aaron's two sons "offered strange fire before the Lord" (Leviticus 10:1–2 KJV). The Bible says, "There went out fire from the Lord and devoured them." Yet again in another account, when the law that God had given His people concerning the handling of the ark of the covenant (Numbers 4:15 KJV) was violated; swift judgment was executed (2 Samuel 6:7 KJV). While transporting the ark back to camp, Uzzah had put his hand on the ark, I presume to stabilize it as the oxen shook the ark. Though assumption is often considered unreliable at best, the thought that I am left with is that Uzzah meant well. Nevertheless, the result of nonconformance, while tragic, was undoubtedly clear to those in the presence of the ark of the covenant of God that day and must have struck great fear into the hearts of all who were present. Truth be told, it strikes fear into my heart just reading of these accounts, knowing how easily and haphazardly I sometimes tend to step to the left or right.

I was raised by an abrasive man, and the thought of being in the presence of a holy God is alarming and stringently sobering, knowing that it is a fearful thing to fall into the hands of the living God. I think the reason it's not, for many of us, is merely a matter of perspective. I'm not referring only to those who are in open rebellion, or defiance, but also to the fence sitters and the backsliders (present company included). The analogy that Dr. Tony Evans used in one of his sermons comes to mind while pondering the concept of man's perspective of God. The following was written to the best of my recollection of the highlights of this analogy an unknown number of years after hearing the sermon.

> If someone were to see a picture of Niagara Falls, you might hear words like *cool, nice,* or *wow.* People might comment on the waterfall and ask when and where the photo was taken. If that same person were to visit Niagara Falls standing at the upper guardrail near the falls taking in the whole experience with all five senses, you might hear stronger worded comments, such as *beautiful, majestic,* or *powerful.* People might try to describe how they were feeling upon their arrival. They might even have gotten that tingly feeling that runs from your spine clear up into the base of the skull and then wraps around the scalp. If they were to purchase tickets to tour the base of the falls on the *Maid of the Mist* and were totally engulfed in the mist, confronted with the massive volume of water, intimidated by the continuous sound pressure, feeling the force of impact of the weight of all that water hitting the rocks, a real up close and personal experience, you might hear even stronger descriptions of the account, or you might hear less as the awe of some things tends

to leave people speechless. The point is the difference of experience based on the perspective of the narrator.

While it was much more grippingly delivered verbally by Dr. Evans, a man whom I believe truly lives out his God-given convictions, the analogy serves as a highly effective illustration of the different levels of intimacy regarding a relationship with the Lord God Almighty. The Bible refers to this as the "measure of faith," (Romans 12:3 KJV) which is ultimately delegated by God. Some people know of a God. Some know Him personally through a self-limiting relationship with the Lord Jesus Christ, paid for with God's own blood. Relatively few have a relationship with the Lord God Almighty, again through the shed blood of the Lord Jesus Christ, and it moves mountains, wards off the most competent of foes, and changes circumstances that we as mere finite humans are absolutely powerless to defend ourselves against. Being this close to the one and only true, living God can be so intimidating as to cause fear and trembling—and it should.

> Wherefore, my beloved, as ye have always obeyed, not as in my presence only, but now much more in my absence, work out your own salvation with fear and trembling. For it is God which worketh in you both to will and to do of his good pleasure. (Philippians 2:12–13 KJV)

> Thou believest that there is one God; thou doest well: the devils also believe, and tremble. (James 2:19 KJV)

These scriptures alone should be enough to convince even the surest of nonbelievers in that these devils can outthink, outmuscle, and outwit any human who ever lived, with the sole exception of Jesus Christ Himself, for He is God; yet they know enough in their understanding of who God really is to tremble at the very thought of Him. Yet in contrast, out of a heart of compassion, God promises to bring comfort to His children intimately, as a mother to her child. In the movie *Radio* with Cuba Gooding Jr., there is a strong emotional display of affection in Radio's response to his mama's second request for a hug that strikes me as a good illustration of the kind of relationship the Lord desires to have with His children.

> As one whom his mother comforteth, so will I comfort you; and ye shall be comforted in Jerusalem. (Isaiah 66:13 KJV)

Realizing that this was written by the prophet Isaiah to the Jewish people, I'm not trying to take things out of context but rather to shed light on the great compassion, loving kindness, and tender mercies of a loving, compassionate God. We, as human beings, have strong tendencies to view God much like we've grown to view our earthly fathers. This will always be an inaccurate representation of God's character in the regard that all earthly fathers are fallible human beings. I'm not entirely sure of how to see Him without that bias as it's nearly impossible to unlearn something that it took us all our lives to learn except to say that the more we yield ourselves to God's word and to living in accordance with the leading of His Spirit, the more of Himself He will reveal to us in an intimate manner. He says, "And ye shall seek me, and find me, when ye shall search for me with all your heart." (Jeremiah 29:13 KJV) I certainly don't claim to have reached this level of intimacy with God as there are multiple areas of my life that He has been patiently working with me on, but I do believe wholeheartedly that it's achievable. Perhaps one of the issues holding me back is perceiving this as an achievable plateau rather than just focusing on an ongoing relationship. As I've heard it said before, "Life's a journey, not a destination."

The Price

ALL OF GOD'S ATTRIBUTES ARE unending and unfailing. In my understanding of the scriptures, there is nothing out of His reach, nothing beyond His control, and aside from denying Himself and/or lying, there is nothing He cannot do. I recall speaking with an intellectually accomplished individual regarding this truth when his jesting question to me was, "Could God ever make a rock so big that He couldn't move it?"

In my embarrassment, I didn't have an answer for him until many days afterward. The answer to that question (which was designed to trip me up intellectually) is, that's not something that God would ever do; it doesn't follow suit with His character. Everything He does has a purpose. He never contradicts Himself. God the Father, God the Son, and God the Spirit are one. They are never in contradiction one to another; Jesus proved that with His strict adherence to the will of the Father while He was here on earth as a man. If God chooses to make an astronomically large rock, it's because He has definite purpose behind that decision. If He decides to move it, then it will do as He says, even rotating about its own axis every twenty-four hours and the revolving around a much larger burning rock of fire every 365 days. It will continue to do so until He says otherwise. There is no contradiction, only purpose accomplished. If, in response to His intelligent design, He decides to create plants, animals, complex ecosystems, and an even more complex society of human beings on that rock, He has great purpose behind that as well. If He, being unwilling to compromise with sin yet still desiring to have an intimate relationship with His creation, decides to leave His home in heaven, live on that rock for thirty-three and a half years as a human being without sin, according to the very laws He ordained many years ago through His own chosen prophets, and offer Himself (Jesus) as a sinless sacrifice to atone for the sins of the very people He created without ever compromising His integrity as the God of all righteousness, I humbly suggest to you that He has great purpose in that as well. In my youth, I used to think that the worst part of the crucifixion for Jesus must have been the physical pain and anguish from the crown of thorns, the nails to the cross, and the sword to His side that He had to endure; not to mention the shame of being the half-naked object of ridicule from His own people. I thought that was what He was lamenting in the garden of Gethsemane when He sweated, as it were, great drops of blood. I didn't understand the depth of what it cost God to give His only Son over to become that which He so clearly has *detested* for all of eternity. It was a cost that was so adequately foreshadowed when God told Abraham to offer his only son as a burnt sacrifice for sin. I can't hardly imagine the deep, heart-wrenching grief He had to bear. My uncle Bob explained to me that for the first and only time in eternity, *God would have contact with sin*. In fact, not only was He going to have contact with sin, but *He was also to become sin* and be crucified because of it. God subjected Himself to all that agony, grief, shame, ridicule, and heartache to satisfy His own law on behalf of humanity. (And almost all things are by the law purged with blood; and without shedding of blood is no remission. Hebrews 9:22 KJV) He did all of this on our behalf willingly, the whole time despising the shame.

> "Eloi, Eloi, lama sabachthani"? Which is, being interpreted, "My God, My God, why hast thou forsaken me"? (Mark 15:34 KJV)

Jesus, in His humanity (theoretically), felt the turning away of the Father, for God cannot look upon sin. The same Man (God) who spoke those words in Mark 15 foretold of this event, as God, long before as recorded in Psalm 22. Jesus hung on the cross for six hours that day, signifying that He did this for man, as man was created on the sixth day. The earth turned black for three hours, three being the number of the Holy Trinity (Father, Son, and Spirit), signifying that it was God who orchestrated this event apart from the earth to once and for all pay for the sin of man. From the sixth hour to the ninth hour, there was darkness upon the face of all the earth as God the Father and God the Spirit turned themselves away from sin as Jesus took upon Himself the sin of the world. When He said, "It is finished," He gave up the ghost, and the veil in the temple of God that separated the Holy of Holies, which is where God dwelt apart from the people, was torn from top to bottom because the ultimate sacrifice for the sin of man had been paid in full with God's own blood, therefore opening up God's salvation to "whosoever will." The scene of the Lord's crucifixion, including the two thieves who were crucified with Him, is said to picture all of humankind hanging in the balance between heaven and earth—those who accept Christ, those who reject Christ, and God Himself in the person of Jesus Christ, who alone paid the price for us all.

> For *there is* one God, and one mediator between God and men, the man Christ Jesus; Who gave himself a ransom for all, to be testified in due time. (1 Timothy 2:5–6 KJV)

That, of course, is not the end of the story. The full gospel includes the miraculous resurrection of Christ from the dead. It is through His resurrection only that we are justified, before God, to have an intimate relationship with the God of all creation.

The Learning Curve

As a young man, shortly after coming to the saving knowledge of the Lord Jesus Christ, I used to think it was a good thing for God to have saved me. I was a good ol' boy, a country boy in a sense, someone God approved of enough to save to the elite future society of heaven. I had found God's favor. I mean, sure, I had done some wrong things in the past, but I didn't think they were really all that bad—at least not worthy of death (or so I thought). I felt as though I had so much to offer God. I've been known to be a mediator. I was somewhat of a musician, or at least I thought so. I had a great sense of humor and knew how to tell a joke well (thanks to Uncle Jim). I also seemed to do well at impersonations, which serves well for illustration purposes. I knew how to be sensitive when I needed or wanted to be. I was almost always sincere and compassionate. I had proved to myself that I could be intelligent and quick-witted when necessary. I was taught by my father to live with passion by a spoken set of moral codes that included truth, honesty, integrity, honor, loyalty, compassion, love, hard work, and a certain amount of pride. These are pillars in life that God would want me to uphold and maintain. In my elevated opinion of prideful self, not having a real moral barometer that I knew of, it was really difficult to navigate among these values amid all the peripheral distractions, namely drugs and alcohol. I knew they were real. I knew they were important. Yet the list of "what ifs" in life continued to grow and add to my already perceived ambiguity. Continuing to pursue life with passion, knowing in the back of my mind that God was there to back me up, I endeavored to remain true to my training and maintain my focus on the objectives my father had given me. There were other unidentified objectives at work in me that I was oblivious of, but I took it all in stride and pressed on. I was going to make God proud. *I couldn't have been more wrong!*

> For thou hast said in thine heart, I will ascend into heaven, I will exalt my throne above the stars of God: I will sit also upon the mount of the congregation, in the sides of the north: I will ascend above the heights of the clouds; I will be like the most High. (Isaiah 14:13–14 KJV)

The fact of the matter is, I had not yet learned the proper perspective of who and what I truly am; the Bible says I am a sinner. In fact, the best possible state that I, or anyone else on the planet, could ever hope to be in is a sinner, saved by the grace of the Lord Jesus Christ. All the attributes that I thought I had to offer God are of absolutely no use to Him without Him.

> But we are *all* as an unclean thing, and all our righteousnesses are as filthy rags; and we all do fade as a leaf; and our iniquities, like the wind, have taken us away. (Isaiah 64:6 KJV)

Our attempt to earn God's favor and/or His salvation apart from Him will always be futile, much like when Adam and Eve attempted to cover themselves with fig leaves when they realized that they were naked because of their sin against a holy God. God knew that their attempt to cover themselves was inadequate, so He provided adequate clothing for them and did so apart from them; to do so, the living had to die as He clothed them with "coats of skins" (Genesis 3:21 KJV). It's not about us; it's never been about us. It's always only ever been about God, His will, His plan, and the advancement of His kingdom; the real question is whether we are going to be a part of all that. According to scripture, there are three things innately present in all human beings since the fall of man that are at enmity (enemies) with God: the lust of the eyes, the lust of the flesh, and the pride of life. (The other objectives referred to earlier have now been identified.) Even when I thought I was wholeheartedly living for God, I was guilty of living by all three of His enemies within myself, and I still am at times. I wanted to satisfy the eyes and the flesh, and prideful beyond measure. I was disobedient to my parents and ultimately to God in so many ways, seeking to selfishly fulfil the desires of the flesh. God has shown me that I, in one way or another, have violated every one of those pillars (in the spoken moral code that I referenced earlier) that I so pridefully believed I had upheld. The fact of the matter is, God sees all our efforts to be worthy of His salvation, in and of ourselves, to be as filthy rags. I continuously feel convicted by this moral dilemma, even though it seems to me that oftentimes it's not so much what we do as it is why we're doing it.

> For I know that in me (that is, in my flesh,) dwelleth no good thing: for to will is present with me; but how to perform that which is good I find not. (Romans 7:18 KJV)

For us to believe that we could earn our salvation would be nothing short of arrogance. If we could earn our own salvation, why would He have willingly given so much? Why would He not just accept the good ones and reject the bad ones? If we could meet the requirement of His righteousness in and of ourselves, why would God have accepted the seemingly misplaced agony, shame, and death that He unequivocally endured on the cross? Contrary to the misconceived notion that there are some good people in this world, because of where *He* set the bar, the "good one's basket" would always be empty.

> For *all* have sinned, and come short of the glory of God. (Romans 3:23 KJV)

Don't get me wrong—I think there are a lot of good-hearted people in this world that I consider good, but what we consider good and evil is much different than the Lord's well-established and -maintained separation between good and evil. The salvation that a holy, sinless God has provided, in and of Himself, could not possibly be earned by sinful man because, with the exception of Jesus Christ Himself, all of humankind is tarnished with sin; it cannot be earned by being baptized, fasting, giving to the poor, being good, feeding the hungry, healing the sick, clothing the naked, or anything that we could do through our own efforts to earn His salvation. The fact that God is perfect in nature and stature and has never compromised with sin in any way only reinforces that *His* requirement for the payment for sin would have to be perfect as well. He would not accept anything less, as illustrated in His requirement of the perfect, spotless lamb sacrifices in the Old Testament that were designed to picture Christ Himself as being God's own spotless Lamb. Jesus was not born into sin like we were. His blood was not tarnished with sin. The immaculate conception that some religious groups believe in is slightly misleading. The real immaculate conception was the one that took place in the body of the virgin Mary and was performed by the Holy Spirit of God, theoretically leaving the hymen intact. Therefore, Christ's blood came from God the Father, perfect, spotless, pure, maintaining His deity as God.

> In the beginning was the Word, and the Word was with God, and the Word was God. (John 1:1 KJV)

> And the Word was made flesh, and dwelt among us, (and we beheld his glory, the glory as of the only begotten of the Father,) full of grace and truth. (John 1:14 KJV)

> Forasmuch as ye know that ye were not redeemed with corruptible things, as silver and gold, from your vain conversation received by tradition from your fathers; But with the precious blood of Christ, as of a lamb without blemish and without spot: Who verily was foreordained before the foundation of the world, but was manifest in these last times for you, Who by him do believe in God, that raised him up from the dead, and gave him glory; that your faith and hope might be in God. (1 Peter 1:18–21 KJV)

God has created us all on the same level playing field with regard to our position and relationship toward Him. Regardless of our wealth, poverty, prestige, or homelessness, we are all born into sin; and knowing God's relentless intolerance concerning sin, we are all incapable of paying that debt. Regardless of where we fall in the hierarchical system of this world, we are all born into selfishness by default. Aside from instinctive knowledge, all a baby knows is what he or she feels. *I'm cold and hungry. Something's just not right in my diaper. I don't feel good.* Yet all babies know ,instinctively, is to cry. It's up to Mom and Dad to determine why and respond accordingly. We learn to follow shiny objects visually. We take our first steps toward something that has captured our interest, like our mother's warm smile, the cookie that Grandpa's holding, the shiny buttons on the DVD player, etc. We learn at an early age, before we can even speak, that we can sometimes manipulate people with our actions to get what we want, like when we cry until Mom walks into the room. Then we start developing preferences, tastes, favorite colors, favorite songs, and TV shows. We start preferring relationships with certain people over others based on likes and dislikes. In our society, we are taught to chase after what we want. If we work hard for it, we deserve to have what we want. All these motives fall into one of the three categories that are enemies with God. With infants and toddlers, barring special needs or complications of abuse, it's normal, expected behavior and certainly understandable. With preadolescents and teenagers, it follows a natural progression and is at least tolerated most of the time. As young adults, we should be able to differentiate between wants and needs, even considering varying rates and degrees of mental and emotional development. Yet, at forty-seven years of age, I still find myself, in the old nature, selfishly chasing the desires of my heart instead of seeking to do God's will with the resources He continuously provides for our family. The only difference between then and now is, instead of shiny objects, Mom's smile, or Grandpa's cookie, it's amplifiers, motorcycles, and four-wheel-drives.

> For the good that I would I do not: but the evil which I would not, that I do. Now if I do that I would not, it is no more I that do it, but sin that dwelleth in me. (Romans 7:19–20 KJV)

An old Indian man was speaking to his grandson one day, explaining to him that he had a black wolf and a white wolf inside him that were constantly at war, fighting with one another daily. The grandson asked, "Which one wins, Grandfather?" To which he replied, "The one I feed the most, Grandson." (paraphrased from an unknown origin)

His Part vs. Our Part

ONE OF THE ISSUES REGARDING Christianity that I have struggled with is not recognizing the fact that there is a difference between salvation and the Christian walk. They are relative to one another yet entirely separate, in that God designed, engineered, and choreographed salvation all by Himself, and our Christian walk is predominantly our responsibility, in response to His lead, neither of which can exist except in response to God's initiating call. When I was younger, any time I sat under preaching or was engaged in "spiritual" conversation or even contemplated spiritual matters in my heart, I perceived it as religion. I learned at a young age to compartmentalize religion apart from sin, and it was in that separation that I spent much of my time riding along on a razor's edge in contemplation of which life to live. I spent a large portion of my life grading myself based on which way I went that day, wondering if I was ever going to be good enough to earn heaven, knowing all along that He was fully aware of my actions and all the thoughts that I entertained, the good, the bad, and the ugly. Though I often recognized the Lord's existence throughout my life, I often didn't recognize my response to Him. The problem with that is that my active involvement with sin would kill my spiritual appetite for growth ("for the wages of sin is death ..." Romans 6:23 KJV). Recognizing that God was responsible for salvation and did it "once and for all" not only made perfect sense in the light of His flawless character, but it also lifted a huge spiritual weight off my shoulders in that I no longer had to try to earn it, and if I can't earn it, it is certain I can do nothing to keep it. God, who is perfect and complete in nature, did it. His work is perfect and complete in nature. Just as it was imputed to Abraham for righteousness because he "believed God," when we "believe God," Christ's righteousness is imputed to us unto salvation; it is a gift, freely given should we choose to accept it, but we cannot earn it or keep it of our own volition.

> And therefore it was imputed to him for righteousness. Now it was not written for his sake alone, that it was imputed to him; but for us also, to whom it shall be imputed, if we believe on him that raised up Jesus our Lord from the dead; who was delivered for our offences, and was raised again for our justification. (Romans 4:22–25 KJV)

Our Christian walk, on the other hand, is primarily our responsibility and is often directly reflected in our lives according to how we respond to God's prompting. I'm taught that God leads us in four ways: the still, small voice of the Holy Spirit that can be heard in the heart, His word, the direction of the local church, and the providence of God (or lack thereof, intermixed with physical hardship designed to encourage us to change our direction when we are living contrary to His will as illustrated in the story of Jonah and the whale). Please don't misunderstand my reference to His will. It's not that I think that He is some taskmaster in heaven micromanaging everything we do, just waiting for us to malfunction so He can drop the hammer on us to assert His authority as God in our lives; to the contrary, there is much liberty in the lives of believers. When God created Adam and Eve, He only gave them one rule really: don't eat of the tree that is in the midst of the garden (the tree of knowledge of good and evil). Even so, in Moses's day He gave them ten, and when Jesus was here, He condensed all Ten Commandments into two: love the Lord your God with all you heart, mind, soul, and strength, and love your neighbor as yourself. They were free to live as they wanted in the rest of the garden, freely eating of all the other trees. Christians are free to live their lives in this world, but there are a few boundaries that He has set in place for our own good that we should be mindful of.

As a Christian, one of the most difficult perplexities that I find in life, in regard to determining God's will, is how to differentiate God's voice and/or the leading of the Holy Spirit apart from all other stimuli that I receive—whether they be thoughts of my own resulting from the mind continually processing information or information involuntarily received from other sources. Some things are blatantly obvious, and no further scrutiny is required. Other things, which aren't so obvious, can be quite frustrating, especially if they are tugging at your emotions and toying with your passions. The enemy of our souls knows all too well how to do that as he and his army have been practicing for roughly six thousand years, since the dawn of humanity. Many years ago, I was considering a life-changing endeavor that was propositioned to me by another. After discussing the details with two others who were directly involved, I headed upstairs to my room to get something. As I put my hand on the ladder to get to the third floor, I heard the word *no*. It was still, small, very clear, direct, and immediate, so much so that I stopped and turned around to see who spoke. I could see and hear, down through the handrail of the stairs to the first floor, those I was just speaking with, and it didn't come from them. I looked around and saw that I was alone on the second floor. It didn't occur to me until much later, but I didn't hear that with my ears. I heard it from within my heart, but it wasn't me. It was most certainly from a source other than myself. To be candid, my motives concerning this endeavor were not entirely pure, and neither was the endeavor directly in line with God's word. I wanted this, but for the wrong reasons. There was nothing externally obvious that I could point to that would definitively specify that the voice I heard that day was God's, but that's what it felt like at the time, and it continues to resonate in my soul.

> My sheep hear my voice, and I know them, and they follow me. (John 10:27 KJV)

It has been a long time since I made the decision to override the one word spoken to me on that day, in love I believe. The problem was that I didn't follow His lead. That was a very unwise move on my part. Speaking from experience, it will develop into an extremely difficult and painful transition spiritually, emotionally, and mentally and often transcends physically if we are unwilling to submit ourselves to the will of a loving God. I don't believe

He said no to stop me from enjoyment, or to keep me from something I wanted. I believe He said no in response to His ability to see the end from the beginning. He knew it was not the best choice for all who were involved. Others, who were directly involved, myself included, have shed many tears over the years because of emotional and financial hardships that many of my decisions have caused; that is a grief that I bear often. Having said all of that, things have somehow worked out during and after all these years, and God continues to bless our family with more than we need or deserve. Romans 8:28 often comes to mind when I ponder this part of our history.

> And we know that all things work together for good to them that love God, to them who are the called according to his purpose. (Romans 8:28 KJV)

God's ability to see the end from the beginning is far beyond my comprehension, but it certainly explains a lot. That's how He could prophesy, through His prophets, so many things in the days of the Old Testament, and we can see clearly that they've come to pass in the New Testament as well as in this present time. That's how He could speak to His prophet John as he penned the book of Revelation things that have not yet happened, and they will happen. While the Lord allowed my decision, and I have been blessed with a beautiful wife and five wonderful children, I should have trusted Him. I think that's what it all boils down to—trust. Do I trust Him? Do I trust that He has my best interest at heart? Do I trust that He always knows best? Do I trust what His word says? Do you? I think this is where some of those earthly father issues come into play. Did I trust my dad, or was I simply trying to gain his acceptance? Should it matter at all? In many cases, people have been wrongfully and deeply hurt by their earthly fathers and may never have the chance or the desire for reconciliation. Those who have suffered through severely traumatic hardships have worked hard to build an emotionally impenetrable wall and would have a very difficult time opening their emotions to a heavenly Father for fear of being hurt or rejected again, and understandably so. I humbly submit, it's not fair to hold a grudge against God for things others may have been responsible for, especially since we are ultimately the recipient of our own grudges, causing yet another self-imposed injustice.

The Battle

GOD KNEW WHEN HE CREATED us that life in this world would be difficult. I believe that is why He so thoughtfully created Eve—someone who could share in the joys, happiness, hardships, troubles, and tears that go along with the mundane affairs of life in this world and still be there to offer the security and nonjudgmental comfort pictured in the intro of Tim McGraw's song "All We Ever Find" (YouTube it). She was someone who could reflect our emotions upon us, who would be there to offer nonjudgmental and compassionate insights on the things in life that have us so dreadfully troubled at times. She is someone to offer whole new perspectives to situations that have us highly confused and perplexed. Have you ever thought yourself into a corner and couldn't find a way out regarding a certain issue in life? I have. It amazes me how my wife can walk up, ask what's wrong, hear the problem, and shed new light onto something in minutes that had me hornswoggled for days. Gentlemen, an otherwise dismal situation can be very enlightened by the wisdom the Lord sees fit to give unto our wives. I thank God for my wife. She has helped me to work through many troubling issues in my life. Aside from the perpetual battle against the environmental elements and the intrinsic emotional rollercoaster that ensues, life is very difficult all by itself. When you throw in the knowledge of difficult relationships, attitudes, acne, idiosyncrasies, taxes, bosses, chicken pox, chickens, insurance, head lice, lawsuits, medical bills, teenagers, shingles, accidents, cancer, rape, AIDS, murder, genocide, tornadoes, hurricanes, terrorists, wars, and atomic bombs, life can be overwhelmingly demanding and has the potential to drive anyone to the breaking point. If that weren't enough, certain beings exist that, if permitted, can overpower us in every way imaginable, and just to complicate matters even more, we can't see them. It's quite intimidating to try to fight against a foe that you can't even see; it's even more frustrating to know that the real battle is not against the flesh and blood that we do see when that's what appears to be causing the entire problem and intensifying the pain.

> For we wrestle not against flesh and blood, but against principalities, against powers, against the rulers of the darkness of this world, against spiritual wickedness in high places. (Ephesians 6:12 KJV)

> For though we walk in the flesh, we do not war after the flesh. (2 Corinthians 10:3 KJV)

Though we have the tendency to look at others as being the source of our pain and suffering, if we take the time to seek God in life's hardships, He can show us that the root of the problem is spiritual; and per Tony Evans's biblical interpretation, spiritual problems can only be addressed with spiritual solutions. If there was a demon that was responsible for all your pain in life standing right in front of you face-to-face, you could swing your fists with fury, throw high kicks to his chest and head, retaliating in sincere indignation, and attempt a final body slam with every fiber of your being in hatred, exerting every ounce of energy that you possess. You would fall to the ground in utter exhaustion and would have hit nothing. He would probably be laughing in amusement because you just cussed and swore, something he's been getting me to do since I was old enough to know what a cuss word was. Your pain is real, that demon is real, the people in your life that he and his cohorts are manipulating to make you miserable are real; but no physical weapon that can be found in this world will connect because he doesn't live in this world. That would be like swinging a light beam or a laser at a pitched baseball; your aim might be perfect every time, but you're never going to hit one out of the park unless you change your choice of weapon. It won't have any effect on that baseball other than a brief enlightenment. Of course, it stands to reason that if the enemy can't be seen, neither can the weapons we need to defend and protect ourselves. When misunderstood, this only seems to add frustration to the weighty issues in our lives that we want answers to. I have a partial understanding of this concept yet admittedly struggle with its application in my life and in the lives of those around me.

> (For the weapons of our warfare are not carnal, but mighty through God to the pulling down of strong holds;) Casting down imaginations and every high thing that exalteth itself against the knowledge of God, and bringing into captivity every thought to the obedience of Christ. (2 Corinthians 10:4–5 KJV)

> Wherefore take unto you the whole armour of God, that ye may be able to withstand in the evil day, and having done all, to stand. Stand therefore, having your loins girt about with truth, and having on the breastplate of righteousness; And your feet shod with the preparation of the gospel of peace; Above all, taking the shield of faith, wherewith ye shall be able to quench all the fiery darts of the wicked. And take the helmet of salvation, and the sword of the Spirit, which is the word of God: Praying always with all prayer and supplication in the Spirit, and watching thereunto with all perseverance and supplication for all saints. (Ephesians 6:13–18 KJV)

I've struggled with seeing consistency in regard to answered and unanswered prayers. Although, having said that, I realize that God probably doesn't see much consistency, in line with His will and word, in my prayer life or my life in general for that matter. I have noticed that, over the years, many of my prayers have been focused on self—things I want or don't want, uncomfortable situations I don't want to suffer through, more money for nice things when I've already been given more than I need. I make requests to the living God over all of creation based on emotional responses that are self-serving in one form or another and am continuously confused and disappointed when I don't get the things I ask God for even though they don't seem like bad requests.

> Ye lust, and have not: ye kill, and desire to have, and cannot obtain: ye fight and war, yet ye have not, because ye ask not. Ye ask, and receive not, because ye ask amiss, that ye may consume it upon your lusts. (James 4:2–3 KJV)

Herein is the inconsistency. Don't get me wrong; I still think we are encouraged to be entirely and consciously transparent to God regarding our hearts' desires. I mean, it's not as though we possess the ability to hide anything from Him anyway. Many of those self-serving requests were granted later in life within the limits of His timeframe; my impatient misinterpretation only exposes my self-seeking nature and immaturity as a Christian. The fact of the matter is, the heart is deceitful above all and desperately wicked. Who can know it (Jeremiah 17:9 KJV)? To acknowledge that to self and God almighty is the first step to reconciliation. To be mindful of that in day-to-day life regarding all decisions large and small could very well make the difference between success and failure in life on this planet as a Christian. I believe God wants us to be mindful of those around us in our prayer lives. Jesus constantly worked miracles in the lives of others, healing them from their physical infirmities and ailments, providing for their personal needs, and increasing their quality of life. In a small portion of the creed or statement of faith of a church I once attended pastored by Mike Lavelle, the phrase "reaching inward, outward, and upward in our sphere of influence" caught my attention. There are legitimate needs all around us. Real people have real issues in life that affect them at the very core of their existence, although most people don't divulge that type of information freely as it is often extremely personal and doing so would expose our vulnerabilities. Imagine the difference it would make if all the Christians on the planet would uphold the needs of those around us in prayer to God almighty, earnestly requesting that He would intervene on their behalf, easing their suffering, bringing them victory over strongholds, healing their infirmities, bringing comfort to their grief, and loving our neighbors as ourselves. The requirement is to place others before ourselves or to die to self and live unto Christ, who always lived for others before Himself. I believe this to be directly in line with His teachings and that He led by example. When Christ walked this earth in the flesh, He was humble in stature. Aside from the fact that it is His very nature as the truth, I believe He purposely took on this form, in the likeness of sinful flesh, to be the proper example of how to live life on this planet, and to do so in such a manner that every human being who follows His lead could effectively live life with the same victory, even as a child. The whole reason He came here was to show us how to appropriately live under the subjection of God, die on the cross as payment for our sins, and be resurrected by God the Father for our justification in His supreme victory and then to sit at the right hand of God the Father and rule with all authority over all of creation. It enables us the ability to effectively live in obedience to God with the understanding of how frail our lives are in regard to the powers that be in this world without succumbing to the temptations proposed by an evil, plotting enemy, recognizing that humility wasn't a suggestion. It was a directive given to us for our own good. God knows how powerful Satan is on a personal level. He created him. God knows that our frames are nothing more than dust with His breath in us. When Satan confronted Jesus during His forty-day fast, he focused on Jesus's physical affections and desires, knowing that the flesh is the weakest link in spiritual warfare. First he tempted Jesus with food, knowing that Jesus would be hungry after not eating for forty days.

> Being forty days tempted of the devil. And in those days he did eat nothing: and when they were ended, he afterward hungered. And the devil said unto him, If thou be the Son of God, command this stone that it be made bread. And Jesus answered him, saying, It is written, That man shall not live by bread alone, but by every word of God. (Luke 4:2–4 KJV)

Second he tempted Him with power, fortune, fame, riches, and glory, knowing that these things are pleasing to the flesh and that Jesus was born into poverty in this world.

> And the devil, taking him up into an high mountain, shewed unto him all the kingdoms of the world in a moment of time. And the devil said unto him, All this power will I give thee, and the glory of them: for that is delivered unto me; and to whomsoever I will I give it. If thou therefore wilt worship me, all shall be thine. And Jesus answered and said unto him, Get thee behind me, Satan: for it is written, Thou shalt worship the Lord thy God, and him only shalt thou serve. (Luke 4:5–8 KJV)

Last, he tempted Jesus with His independence to act in pride apart from God the Father's direction and exercise His authority as the Son of God, and he did so attempting to use God's own word against Him.

> And he brought him to Jerusalem, and set him on a pinnacle of the temple, and said unto him, If thou be the Son of God, cast thyself down from hence: For it is written, He shall give his angels charge over thee, to keep thee: And in their hands they shall bear thee up, lest at any time thou dash thy foot against a stone. And Jesus answering said unto him, It is said, Thou shalt not tempt the Lord thy God. (Luke 4:9–12 KJV)

Jesus resisted and defeated the devil using the word of God. It is only after that same manner that we can effectively resist the devil, using God's word, all the while taking great care not to be boastful, prideful, or arrogant, knowing that the devil knows God's word far better than we do.

> For by grace are ye saved through faith; and that not of yourselves: it is the gift of God: Not of works, *lest any man should boast*. (Ephesians 2:8–9 KJV)

Some interesting facts regarding these scriptural accounts are the supernatural ability of Satan to show Jesus all the kingdoms of the earth in a moment of time and the fact that Satan has been given the dominion of the earth (or) the control of this earth has been "delivered to" him, and to whom he will give it. It only stands to reason that we as human beings should be as humble as humanly possible in this foreign land, which is not our home, and with thanksgiving in our hearts, let our requests be made known to "the God of *all* creation" in our quest to live for His purposes. I suppose the most logical question at this point would be, what are His purposes? One of the most recognizable attributes of Jesus was His compassion toward others regardless of their status in this world. It was completely obvious in His teachings, parables, and sermons. His main concern, secondary only to His reverence for the Father, was for His fellow man, for their salvation first but also for their physical, mental, and emotional wellbeing.

> The first of all the commandments is, Hear, O Israel; The Lord our God is one Lord: And thou shalt love the Lord thy God with all thy heart, and with all thy soul, and with all thy mind, and with all thy strength: this is the first commandment. And the second is like, namely this, Thou shalt love thy neighbour as thyself. There is none other commandment greater than these. (Mark 12:29–31 KJV)

He demonstrated His compassion for others by feeding them in large multitudes, turning water into the finest of wines at a joyful occasion, healing the sick, and causing the lame to walk, the blind to see, and the dead to be raised to life. He showed His love for others by being concerned for their lives and offered His amazing grace to those who suffered emotionally like the woman at the well and Mary of Magdalene, even to the point of healing the ear that the apostle Peter cut off in Jesus's own defense, which belonged to the man who came to arrest Jesus and take Him to the courts that would deliver Him to the cross. It's clear to me that His concern was not only the salvation of our souls but our personal well-being as well, as expressed in His request of the Father to "forgive them, for they know not what they do." So I suppose in retrospect, the logical conclusion would be that our purpose as believers is to follow His lead—love the Lord God with all our hearts, minds, strength, and souls, bring honor and glory to God, and worship Him in Spirit and truth with a lifestyle of worship. Love others, regardless of their status in life, with the same deep, heartfelt compassion Jesus has shown us while He was here on earth in the flesh. Endeavor to lead others to Christ, the God of all comfort. Encourage the body of Christ, feed the hungry, cloth the naked, shelter the homeless, encourage the downtrodden, and forgive those who repent. All these things can be accomplished out of a pure heart of gratefulness for all the things the Lord has done and continues to do for us.

> Thou shalt love the Lord thy God with all thy heart, and with all thy soul, and with all thy mind. This is the first and great commandment. And the second *is* like unto it, Thou shalt love thy neighbour as thyself. On these two commandments hang all the law and the prophets. (Matthew 22:37–40 KJV)

These two commandments don't cancel or diminish the Ten Commandments given to Moses back in Exodus 20 in the Old Testament in any way, but they will fulfil them if strictly adhered to. The first four of the Ten Commandments were directly in line with the first commandment Jesus gave us regarding that vertical relationship between man and the Lord God Almighty.

> Thou shalt have no other gods before me. Thou shalt not make unto thee any graven image, or any likeness of any thing that is in heaven above, or that is in the earth beneath, or that is in the water under the earth. Thou shalt not bow down thyself to them, nor serve them: for I the LORD thy God am a jealous God, visiting the iniquity of the fathers upon the children unto the third and fourth generation of them that hate me; And showing mercy unto thousands of them that love me, and keep my commandments. Thou shalt not take the name of the LORD thy God in vain; for the LORD will not hold him guiltless that taketh his name in vain. Remember the sabbath day, to keep it holy. Six days shalt thou labor, and do all thy work: But the seventh day is the sabbath

> of the LORD thy God: in it thou shalt not do any work, thou, nor thy son, nor thy daughter, thy manservant, nor thy maidservant, nor thy cattle, nor thy stranger that is within thy gates: For in six days the LORD made heaven and earth, the sea, and all that in them is, and rested the seventh day: wherefore the LORD blessed the sabbath day, and hallowed it. (Exodus 20:1–4 KJV)

The next six were regarding the horizontal relationship between man and those around him (or his neighbors).

> Honor thy father and thy mother: that thy days may be long upon the land which the LORD thy God giveth thee. Thou shalt not kill. Thou shalt not commit adultery. Thou shalt not steal. Thou shalt not bear false witness against thy neighbor. Thou shalt not covet thy neighbor's house, thou shalt not covet thy neighbor's wife, nor his manservant, nor his maidservant, nor his ox, nor his ass, nor any thing that is thy neighbor's. (Exodus 20:5–10 KJV)

When Jesus was here, as a man He experienced all the negative emotions that we do. He has known on a personal level exactly what it means to be cold, frustrated, sweaty, hungry, tired, in pain, rejected, despised, ridiculed, beaten, abused, spit on, betrayed, and murdered; in addition to that, He has been tempted in every way we have. He cried heartfelt tears of sorrow concerning the death of Lazarus for those around Him, even knowing that He was about to bring him back to life; He identified with their heartache.

> For we have not an high priest which cannot be touched with the feeling of our infirmities; but was in all points tempted like as *we are, yet* without sin. (Hebrews 4:15 KJV)

I firmly believe in His ability to identify with each of us in our individual struggles in life regardless of what the situation may be. I feel as though I am without excuse when it comes to the question of my loyalty to Him and His cause, and yet I am still burdened with guilt at times because of the lack thereof.

> Not that I speak in respect of want: for I have learned, in whatsoever state I am, therewith to be content. Both how to be abased, and I know how to abound: everywhere and in all things I am instructed both to be full and to be hungry, both to abound and to suffer need. (Philippians 4:11–12 KJV)

Also, I find it noteworthy that Jesus never ran. He walked. To put it in other words, He didn't get in a big hurry and rush into things and do them haphazardly. He did all things at a steady pace with specific purpose in mind, to the best of His human ability I'm sure. He is our example.

> Looking unto Jesus the author and finisher of our faith; who for the joy that was set before him endured the cross, despising the shame, and is set down at the right hand of the throne of God. (Hebrews 12:2 KJV)

He showed us the life of obedience. He taught us how to live in subjection under God, but for years I completely missed the why behind it all. Why did He live the life He did when it would have been so much easier to just live like everyone else was living? How did He stay firm when He felt like giving up? It was for the joy that was set before Him. That is the mark that Paul writes about in Philippians 3:14. It's the same joy that caused Paul and Silas to sing praises to God while they were in prison. That is the fuel that should feed the flames of passion in our hearts to live in accordance to the will of God, the joy of His salvation—the reason we press toward the mark for the prize of the high calling of God in Christ Jesus; the way to obtain, through His grant, the peace of God that passes all understanding. I think herein is the vehicle that transports us through faith unto victory. I'm being slightly hypocritical as I don't function efficiently with regard to this premise, but I am learning day by day that when I respond to the pieces of truth that God gives me and begin to function accordingly, He then continues to give me more truth to follow. That joy is initially given to us when we trust God for salvation.

I can remember shortly after grasping the reality of His salvation waking up one morning literally singing, "Turn your eyes upon Jesus." It just flowed from inside my heart. I could hardly contain myself; it permeated every fiber of my being. I know now that this is what Peter meant by "joy unspeakable and full of glory." The joy of the Lord is powerful. It can transform the shakiest of lives. It has transformed some of the most seemingly contrary lives on the planet. The apostle Paul took great pride in persecuting and murdering Christians, yet after his transformation, he wrote a large part of the New Testament that, since then, has in turn transformed hundreds of thousands, perhaps millions, maybe even billions of lives over the past two thousand years. I'm told that John Newton was known to be a ruthless taskmaster in the slave trade industry in the Royal Navy and was so vile that his own crew committed mutiny by throwing him overboard; yet after his conversion, he wrote one of the most heartwarming hymns of all time, "Amazing Grace." It's probably been sung in every church in the world by now and speaks intimately to many believers. The joy of the Lord is far greater than any drug on the planet. It has lasting effects on all the lives He blesses with it. There is a catch though. Sin diminishes the joy that He gives us. Certain things need to be in alignment for us to reap the full benefits of the joy of His salvation. We need to be living for His purposes, performing in accordance with His will in our lives, reading His word to know what His will is. We must take time for prayer on a regular basis to communicate with Him those things that concern us and allow Him the opportunity to communicate to us the things we need to know regarding our situation in life. Keeping ourselves unspotted from the world of sin is a huge factor in my opinion. As I see it, the more we submit ourselves to Him, the more of His will for our lives He reveals to us. His joy is a wonderful inspirational bonus that can lead us into the paths of righteousness when we submit ourselves to His revealed truth.

The Spirit Realm

EVEN THOUGH THE LORD CAN identify with us, and the Holy Spirit resides in our hearts, the devil still knows how to attack us. He is monumentally intelligent, cunning, and crafty. To think that our names haven't come up in heavenly conversations among the good and the evil would be a naïve, total miscalculation of facts on our part. This is a *war*! He is considered the "accuser of the brethren." I've been told that we all have a guardian angel that watches over us.

> Are they not all ministering spirits, sent forth to minister for them who shall be heirs of salvation? (Hebrews 1:14 KJV)

That being true, you could almost bet that the opposing side has appointed a member or two to watch you, study you, study your responses, monitor your speech, throw things at you, and watch what sticks. The spirit world seems to be where the real battles exist as well as the real powers. Angels and demons alike have superior physical strength, when manifested in this physical world, as well as a seemingly endless supply of resources, yet only as God permits, on both sides. In Mark 5:4, people tried to bind the demon-possessed man from the Gadarenes with chains and fetters and he "plucked them asunder." Having worked with steel for much of my career, I can attest that it takes an enormous amount of force, in comparison to soft flesh and brittle bone, to break steel. It is my firm belief that the strongest, most intelligent human being is no match physically, mentally or spiritually, for angelic or demonic beings. Though the spiritual realm seems to coexist with and be directly linked to the physical realm, this fourth dimension that we cannot detect with any of the five physical senses of the human *body seems to be a superhighway for angelic and demonic beings alike, where much of the war* between good and evil rages on. The ninth verse in Jude describes a dispute over the body of Moses between Michael, the archangel of God, and the devil. Job 1:6 says the devil was permitted in with the sons of God to present themselves before the Lord. It doesn't specify whether either of these two events took place in the spirit realm or in the natural world as we know it, yet it isn't much of a stretch to believe that, as God resides in heaven, the latter may very well have been in the spirit realm. The dispute was over the physical body of Moses; with that in mind, it only makes sense that spirit beings have the knowledge and ability to alter their matter on somewhat of a molecular level to be able to manipulate people or objects in the physical realm. The point is that there is much more to the big picture than what we can see, hear, feel, taste, and smell in the natural world. In an Old Testament account when the Lord's prophet, Elisha, was surrounded by an army on a mission to subdue him, his protégé was fear struck.

> And Elisha prayed, and said, Lord, I pray thee, open his eyes, that he may see. And the Lord opened the eyes of the young man; and he saw: and, behold, the mountain was full of horses and chariots of fire round about Elisha. (2 Kings 6:17 KJV)

The mountain was full of horses and chariots of fire in the spirit world before the servant's eyes were opened. It's just that he was unaware of it until the Lord allowed him to see into the spirit world. The realm that God's kingdom primarily operates in seems to be unending, with inexhaustible resources, and is typically invisible to the human eye (ultimate reality). This spiritual realm may be what scientists are calling dark matter and dark energy.

> NASA states, "More is unknown than is known. We know how much dark energy there is because we know

how it affects the universe's expansion. Other than that, it is a complete mystery. But it is an important mystery. It turns out that roughly 68% of the universe is dark energy. Dark matter makes up about 27%. The rest - everything on Earth, everything ever observed with all of our instruments, all normal matter - adds up to less than 5% of the universe. Come to think of it, maybe it shouldn't be called "normal" matter at all, since it is such a small fraction of the universe." (https://science. nasa.gov/astrophysics/focus-areas/what-is-dark-energy, Bradley Young)

I've heard of accounts from children and adults alike of beings appearing to walk through walls or just "appearing" in a room; after the crucifixion of the Lord Jesus Christ, when the apostles were gathered together in the upper room with the doors closed, Christ appeared. In theory, if the best science of our day is right, all our best scientists can detect with the most sophisticated technology we have makes up just under 5 percent of all there is in existence. In accordance to the Bible, it is Christ who created all things physical and spiritual, and He has been given sovereign authority over all by God the Father.

> For by Him were all things created, that are in heaven, and that are in earth, visible and invisible, whether they be thrones, or dominions, or principalities, or powers: all things were created by Him, and for him: And He is before all things, and by Him all things consist. (Colossians 1:16–17 KJV)

When He walked this earth, He demonstrated His authority in Mark 4:39 by bringing the weather into subjection with the power of His word when He said, "Peace, be still" and the storm was immediately calmed and also in the account of the demons that Christ had ordered out of the man in Mark 5:1–13 as they requested of the Lord to allow them to enter the swine. They recognized His authority as the Son of God.

"What have I to do with thee, Jesus, thou Son of the most high God? I adjure thee by God, that thou torment me not." (Mark 5:7 KJV)

Satan himself was given permission, by God, to destroy Job's family, cattle, and crops and did so in one day—though he could only do that which God permitted him to do. The record also states that God restored double unto Job for his obedience to and faith in God through this tragic experience. The kingdom of heaven has been at war with the kingdom of hell since the fall of Satan. It is a spiritual battle that bleeds over into the physical realm moment by moment. All the miracles that Moses performed, at God's bidding, while trying to convince the pharaoh to let God's people go, were duplicated by the pharaoh's (the devil's) magicians *except for one.* When God, through Moses, turned the dust of the earth into lice (living organisms) in Exodus 8:16–19, the devil's own magicians told the pharaoh, *"This is the finger of God."* I also think it's interesting to note that the only thing they could not duplicate was the original creation of life from the dust of the earth, which is exactly what we were created from. When Moses and the magicians threw their staffs onto the ground, they became serpents, though it's interesting that Moses's serpent ate the magician's serpents. One could argue that the staffs were dead wood, yet we know from the resurrection of Lazarus, Jesus, and all those who were resurrected with Christ, that God has the power to raise the dead and alter His creation of life as He sees fit. We know from that same account as well as the one in the book of Revelation that the devil has been given power to restore life and alter it.

Jesus said unto her, I am the resurrection, and the life. (John 11:25 KJV)

And I saw one of his heads as it were wounded to death; and his deadly wound was healed. (Revelations 13:3 KJV)

The enemy of our souls has been given unimaginable power, strength, and ability and is using his resources to deceive as many as possible into denying the one true God and worshiping the beast. In accordance to the book of Revelation, Satan is planning to set himself up in the temple of God to be worshiped as God in complete, blatant defiance of God (referenced in Mathew and Mark as the abomination of desolation). He is working hard to crumble the kingdoms of this world into a new world order with one government, one currency, and one leader ... himself. Many countries are falling apart, including this one. America has been under spiritual attack for many years, and it is beginning to manifest in the losing of her freedoms as she is swiftly being transformed into a socialist country by sleight of hand, smoke, and mirrors. Greece was recently bankrupt with an all-time high in male suicide. Civil unrest and violence in Africa continue to plague the nation. Russia suffers from a dependency that has the potential to spiral them into a societal collapse. Drug-related wars and civil violence continue to plague Mexico and South America. Wars rage on in many other countries. There has been an increase in the frequency of catastrophic events and natural disasters, flooding, hurricanes, tsunamis, sinkholes, tornadoes, mud-slides ... Imagine for a moment, with the world falling apart at an ever-increasing rate of speed, and a prestigious individual shows up on the scene who can speak every language on the planet, performing miracles and wonders that can only seemingly be rivaled or mimicked with Hollywood's knack for special effects, with answers to seemingly all of man's problems, performing signs and wonders in the skies. What do you suppose the world is going to think? This is Satan's plan: to be worshiped as God. He is using all the resources available to him, including those in the spiritual realm, to assist him in manipulating human beings, families, neighborhoods, cities, states, provinces, and countries on this earth into denying God and worshiping him. He was convincing enough to con one-third of the angels in heaven into abandoning their first estate, and their Maker, into following him. I suppose, in a manner of speaking, God is Satan's Father just as He is our Father. He created him just as He created us. Though God hates sin, I still believe that He loves His creation; and although He may not have used the dust of this earth to create the devil, I do find it interesting that the Bible describes the physical characteristics of the devil as being made up of elements deemed of value that we mine out of the earth. Additionally, *in my imagination*, I can picture God creating the "covering cherub" described in the scriptures below, a magnificently dynamic, absolutely stunning, and exceptional creature with unsurpassed beauty that emits a brilliant countenance brightly reflected by the precious stones in his covering using his many sets of wings to fly over the throne of God in adoration, praise, and worship of God the Father, creating beautiful, harmonious music with pipes built into his massively powerful wings by varying the speed of hummingbird-like reciprocation and engaging with sequential precision the numerous fleshlike valves, built into his pipes controlling tonal characteristics, harmonies, and kaleidoscopic melodies in perfect composition with flawless timing signatures from tabrets integrated into his complex physique, varying the intensity of his countenance to the rhythm of the music he produces. As alluded to earlier, much of that comes from my imagination intermixed with some facts from the Bible. Perhaps one of the reasons the God of all creation allows the devil to propagate evil on the planet is for a system of checks and balances against all who reject Him as well as those of us who contemplate rubbing that upper limit from time to time.

> Thus saith the Lord GOD; Thou sealest up the sum, full of wisdom, and perfect in beauty. Thou hast been in Eden the garden of God; every precious stone was thy covering, the sardius, topaz, and the diamond, the beryl, the onyx, and the jasper, the sapphire, the emerald, and the carbuncle, and gold: the workmanship of thy tabrets and of thy pipes was prepared in thee in the day that thou wast created. Thou art the anointed cherub that covereth; and I have set thee so: thou wast upon the holy mountain of God; thou hast walked up and down in the midst of the stones of fire. Thou wast perfect in thy ways from the day that thou wast created, till iniquity was found in thee. (Ezekial 28:12–15 KJV)

Know this: it is the all-knowing, all-seeing mind of God (Father) in constant communion with His own heart (Spirit) that speaks the word (Son) and controls the hand (Son) that holds the chain that limits the devil that controls his minions who influence the people and creatures that are in your world and surround you and those you love, day by day moment by moment, down to the scrutiny of a subatomic level. The laws of sowing and reaping are intrinsically wired into God's creation. They are automatic, all-inclusive, and all-encompassing. They never sleep. They never rest. Though I don't doubt the ability of God to maintain perfect dominion over His creation in accordance with His permissive will, from my minuscule perspective, that certainly is one intimidating creature; and no matter how tough, bad, or evil anyone on this planet thinks he or she is, he or she is in no wise even close to being the slightest threat to a being of this magnitude who, by the way, has no conscience.

began working on a bottle of wine and possibly some other natural mood enhancers. Our mother was preparing dinner on the grill, while my brother and I just kind of hung out. Mom was praising the Lord for the trip, thanking God for the camping gear, the weather, the fishing poles ... just about anything you could think of really. Well, Dad became a little irritated with this as he was a professed nonbeliever at the time and momentarily predisposed to a slightly different mind-set. Dad was generally outspoken about everything. So, as Mom continued, he interrupted to inform her that God didn't provide the camping equipment—the credit union did, and he was making payments on all of it. Unmoved by this, Mom continued to thank God for His provisions.

As Dad was distracted from his conversation again, he grew more brazen and interrupted Mom again, questioning her, "If your God is so great, how come He forgot to have me pack a shovel so we could dig up some worms to fish with?"

Well, Mom didn't have an answer for him, so she continued passively with dinner in silence. After an early dinner, Dad felt the need to answer nature's call. He looked around and spotted a small group of trees about fifty yards or so off in the distance. In the interest of being modest, as there were other campers in the area, he decided to make the walk. As his water began to displace the soil, he could see something being revealed beneath the dirt; unable to make out the shape as it was growing dark, he reached down to pick up an old collapsible military shovel. Can you imagine the look of utter shock on his face? When he returned with shovel in hand, his jaw was kind of hanging. I remember many years of praying with my brother and my mom for Dad's salvation. It didn't mean as much to me then as I didn't understand what that was all about really, but it speaks volumes to me now. God, who knows the end from the beginning, knew that shovel was there as well as the person who left it there. He saw fit to use that knowledge to get the attention of and put to silence the ramblings of an intoxicated man. Dad did eventually respond to God's offer of salvation, and that shovel remained in our home for the rest of Dad's life and must have been a constant reminder to him that nothing on this planet is outside of God's reach or knowledge. I've heard him tell that story many times and always with a sense of awe. I've used the terms *molecular* and *subatomic levels* a couple of times in this book. When Dad walked to a gathering of trees, he was under the influence; he thought it was his idea to walk to that destination. I believe the Lord directed him without him knowing it. Perhaps the Lord put the idea of a shovel in his mind even knowing his contempt of spirit. God is gracious. When the Lord hardened the pharaoh's heart, I'm sure he had not even the slightest inclination that God was behind it. I am convinced that God is so plugged in to his creation that He is often in our minds and we are unaware of His presence on this regard. That seems to me to be on a molecular level.

> O lord, thou hast searched me, and known me. Thou knowest my downsitting and mine uprising, thou understandest my thought afar off. Thou compassest my path and my lying down, and art acquainted with all my ways. For there is not a word in my tongue, but, lo, O Lord, thou knowest it altogether. Thou hast beset me behind and before, and laid thine hand upon me. Such knowledge is too wonderful for me; it is high, I cannot attain unto it. Whither shall I go from thy spirit? or whither shall I flee from thy presence? If I ascend up into heaven, thou art there: if I make my bed in hell, behold, thou art there. If I take the wings of the morning, and dwell in the uttermost parts of the sea; Even there shall thy hand lead me, and thy right hand shall hold me. If I say, Surely the darkness shall cover me; even the night shall be light about me. Yea, the darkness hideth not from thee; but the night shineth as the day: the darkness and the light are both alike to thee. For thou hast possessed my reins: thou hast covered me in my mother's womb. I will praise thee; for I am fearfully and wonderfully made: marvellous are thy works; and that my soul knoweth right well. (Psalm 139:1–14 KJV)

Shortly after my wife had given birth to our youngest daughter, the hospital informed us that she would have to stay in the hospital in an incubator until her statistics improved to acceptable levels as she was born four and a half months premature and only weighed one pound, eight ounces, at birth. I remember she was so small she could fit in the palm of my hand, and she came out fighting. After what would have been a normal gestation period, the hospital gave us an oxygen bottle, a baby monitor, and some inhalants for her lungs and sent us home. After the sixth day, she stopped breathing and was life-flighted back to the hospital in Cleveland. The doctors and nurses did everything humanly possible to save that little girl, but everything they did, her body seemed to reject. It was quite a sight to see that little infant in the middle of that great big bed with all those tubes and wires leading away from her body to the machines that were bigger than I was and wrapped halfway around the bed. The breathing machine that she was on would provide oxygen mechanically. When she would try to breathe on her own, the breathing machine would add air, exceeding the capacity of her lungs, forcing holes in her lung linings and filling the chest cavity between the lung and chest with fluid, producing pneumothoraxes in two different places and in turn preventing her lungs from being able to expand. Incisions were made to drain off the fluid and allow her lungs to expand. After days of numerous failed attempts to restore her health, they called two other hospitals that specialized in premature lung disease, one in Michigan, and one in California, both of which declined her as her stats were already below the presumed point of no return. The look in the doctor's eyes confirmed what he was trying so desperately not to say. With our other four children spread out at babysitters in different areas of the state and numerous trips back and forth, we were given a room to stay at for a few days until the expected inevitable event took place. My wife and I were in total bewilderment in what seemed like a hopeless situation. We held each other, but comfort seemed to evade us. I curled up in the corner of the bathroom floor off to the side of the NICU and cried, asking God to either give her back to us or to take her home to Him. After a few more attempts at comfort, we went to bed that night expecting the worst.

You can imagine our surprise when the doctor came into the room in the morning and said, "Mr. Willett, we don't understand it because medically speaking this doesn't happen, but her lungs seem to be repairing themselves."

With a locked gaze, I pointed upward; he responded with raised eyebrows and a tilted nod before departing. Did God answer my prayers?

Did God answer the many other prayers of Christians more obedient than I? Why did God save my daughter when so many others more deserving than I who have prayed just as hard with tears that were just as real have lost their dear, precious children? I cannot answer these questions. With tears in my eyes and a grateful heart, I can only attest that my daughter is now a beautiful young woman of twenty-three years, who, against all odds given to us by the experts, is very much alive and still a fighter. One thing I am sure of is that as undeserving as I am for God to have moved on our behalf, His grace has prevailed miraculously. Would He have done so if we had not prayed? I suppose because He has a specific plan for her here on earth, He still would have saved her regardless of our response; but I believe we can bend God's ear (so to speak).

Many years ago, my wife and I lived approximately forty minutes away from my work. I enjoyed my job at the time as it seemed to be an answer to prayer. One day on the way home, the engine blew up, leaving me stranded. I was unsure of what to make of it all as I still needed to be at work every day. Not having much money to speak of, I was quite perplexed as to what to do and was concerned about losing my job. My wife and I knelt at our bed, held hands, and prayed together regarding the matter at hand. I can't remember the entire prayer word for word, but I do remember the basics of it as being the following: "Lord, Your word says that You're an ever-present help in time of need, and I need You now. God, I need a car. You provided this job for me in an answer to prayer, for which I'm grateful, and now I have no way to get there. And," I prayed with a small chuckle, "so long as You're going to provide us a car, can you make it a nice-looking one?"

At the time, I didn't expect to receive a direct answer. I expected to limp along borrowing vehicles from family members until I ran across some affordable beater somewhere and bought another set of problems to work on over the weekends. My wife's father loaned me his truck for a couple of weeks to get by. On my way home from work one day, I decided to go to the little village shopper for something and caught a glimpse of a very attractive Oldsmobile, Buick Regal out of the corner of my eye, and it had a "For Sale" sign in the window. I practically gave myself whiplash turning to see it. After seeing it, I thought to myself, *They're going to want a lot of money for that* and continued to the store. On the return trip, I thought, *Well, maybe I could offer them some kind of payment plan. The worst they can say is no...* I knocked on the door, and the woman told me that her and her husband invested a large amount of money into restoring the car to pristine condition, only to find that the new engine they recently put in it had started knocking. In their disgust, they decided to sell it and pursue another project. She was a little shocked that I stopped as she had just put the sign on it not long before I showed up, but she said that if I had $250, I could have it. I was in disbelief for a little while, but I beamed with joy as I drove that car, knock and all, for quite some time after that. It was gorgeous. With a fresh, shiny black paint job and red pinstripes near the upper corners of the fenders with red plush interior, it even smelled like a new car. I can't remember exactly how long it was, but I sold that car to an acquaintance about a year or so later and it still ran, with the same knock. Folks, God answered that prayer to the very details that we prayed into it, even to the part that I was being facetiously selfish about.

Some time after that, I once again found myself without a vehicle while living in the same house and working the same job. While the fellow with the tow truck was picking up a truck with a sick engine from my driveway, I was telling him of my predicament. After he left, I remembered God's answer to our last prayer concerning a vehicle and requested of my wife to come pray with me again. The prayer was just for reliable transportation this time as I thought I was pushing my luck if I asked for more. This time it was less than an hour before Scotty, the tow truck driver, called me, saying, "You're not going to believe this but ..." It was a Pontiac, and although not nearly as attractive as the first answer to prayer, it was certainly a reliable source of transportation and kept our family mobile for a good stretch of time.

Our grandmother was a beautiful woman from the inside out; her truthful spirit permeated throughout her entire being in sincerity and love. She was loyally devoted to her family in every way imaginable. She served up dinner to Grandpa every evening in the living room, complete with his own dinner tray, salt shaker, and cold glass of beer with a frothy head. She kept her house in the cleanest of order. I remember when I was a young boy she often took the time out of her busy day to write letters to her grandson expressing to him her warm devotion with the utmost of respect as she gave him the written title of "Master" preceding his name on the envelope. Although at the time I never understood why she gave me that title, it sure made a huge difference in the life of that little boy and made him feel good about himself—a commodity that was far too often missing in action. I learned a great deal in my correspondence with her, things that will live in me for the rest of my life; but I think the one thing that stands out the most is her sincerity. Grandma always told us, "You get out of life what you put into it." The Bible says it slightly different, although it carries with it the added gravity of God's supreme authority, but the principal meaning is the same.

> Be not deceived; God is not mocked: for whatsoever a man soweth, that shall he also reap. (Galatians 6:7 KJV)

One of the things Grandma told me, in regard to matters of faith, made more sense to me than I've heard from most others I've conversed with on the topic. She told me one time that she learned more in the last three years of reading the Bible at home than she did in more than twenty years of attending her church. Now I don't necessarily believe that means we shouldn't attend church, as I believe the Bible directs us otherwise. I do believe that it speaks volumes as to the power unleashed from God's word in contrast to man's social and structured events regardless of what title or denomination we label them with. That being written, there is a clear contrasting difference between a man of God, living out the purpose of God, filled with the Spirit of God, preaching the word of God, as compared to a social gathering, again regardless of the label.

> Not forsaking the assembling of ourselves together, as the manner of some is; but exhorting one another: and so much the more, as ye see the day approaching. (Hebrews 10:25 KJV)

It was entirely clear in more than one of the poems she wrote in her later years in life, one of which was entitled, "My Friend." It was in that poem that I realized that Grandma knew God on a personal level intimately. Out of eight children, she suffered through the loss of two of them taken at a young age. She also suffered the loss of two husbands. Of a certainty, she was acquainted with grief and heartache; but she knew the Lord, who saw her through that grief and gave her hope to move on in faith one step at a time. I firmly believe she currently resides in heaven with Him.

I believe wholeheartedly that God loves us and in His goodness is willing to reflect His concern about the things we are concerned about, but we need to communicate those things to Him. The Bible is peppered throughout its history with stories of specific answers to prayer in detail. God has not changed. He still interacts and relates to man in the same way as in biblical times. After the Lord's crucifixion, there were two men walking down the road, and they were overwhelmed over what happened to their Lord on the cross. As their resurrected Lord started walking beside them, He asked them why they were so distraught, to which they responded, not knowing that it was Him, "Man, where have you been? Haven't you seen what they've done to our Lord, how He was crucified and buried in the tomb?" (paraphrased from Luke 24 beginning at verse 13). As they walked along, the Lord encouraged them with quotes from the holy Scriptures. As they began to be encouraged, they turned aside to go into their home. When they turned, the Lord kept walking on; when they saw that it was the Lord who encouraged them, they asked Him to come in and sup with them (have dinner). He responded to their request by entering their home and spending time with them in fellowship. The point is, God is going to continue right on being God in all His glory; if we take the time to ask of Him things that we are concerned with, He can and often does respond accordingly. If we don't, He doesn't have reason to. The Bible tells us with thanksgiving in our hearts, let our requests be made known unto God. In short, that's prayer.

> Let us therefore come boldly unto the throne of grace, that we may obtain mercy, and find grace to help in time of need. (Hebrews 4:16 KJV)

> Let your moderation be known unto all men. The Lord *is* at hand. Be careful for nothing; but in everything by prayer and supplication with thanksgiving let your requests be made known unto God. And the peace of

God, which passeth all understanding, shall keep your
hearts and minds through Christ Jesus. (Philippians
4:5–7 KJV)

I'm reminded of the lyrics to that beautiful hymn, "What a friend we
have in Jesus"

O what peace we often forfeit, O what needless pain we bear,
All because we do not carry everything to God in prayer.

Have we trials and temptations? Is there trouble anywhere?
We should never be discouraged; take it to the Lord in
prayer.
Can we find a friend so faithful who will all our sorrows
share?
Jesus knows our every weakness; take it to the Lord in
prayer.

Are we weak and heavy laden, cumbered with a load of
care?
Precious Savior, still our refuge, take it to the Lord in prayer.

I'm convinced that those words, as well as what probably equates to
billions of other hymns and songs, were penned by God's people through
the wisdom brought on by suffering and personal experience of intimacy
with a God who truly cares but is unwilling to compromise with sin.
When I think of all the details surrounding our daughter's brush with
death, it amazes me, after the fact, that I can see how God was there all
along choreographing all the events that led up to that entire experience.
Prior to a time when moments would really count, God made provision.
My wife is very intelligent. She remembers things precisely to the finest
of details. Though she isn't always right, I've learned to trust in her
ability to be accurate over the last twenty-five years, believe me. She
remembered that the baby had an eye doctor appointment on Wednesday.
That's significant for two reasons in that we lived an hour away from
the hospital, and she remembered the right appointment on the wrong
date; I find that rather ironic in that I've lost many an argument because

of her keen awareness and remarkable memory. We drove to Cleveland, and I dropped her and our daughter off at my mom's apartment and went to work. Upon returning to Mom's apartment after work, we noticed that the baby monitor began beeping, and Dehlia was unresponsive and turning bluish in color, which started the entire chain of events described earlier. Had my wife not remembered wrongly, we would have been an hour away from the hospital and staff that was familiar with her situation, again when moments really counted. I was clueless when He was not. I've shared these experiences because I remember when I was highly skeptical concerning a real relationship between God and man, even some time after I professed to believe.

When the Lord was on earth as a man, He often spoke in parables. Parables are an earthly picture used to describe a heavenly principle or word pictures. I believe there are many of those pictures still available today that can effectively be used for the purposes of illustration. My father used to call them God's fingerprints—little trace amounts of evidence that point to God's involvement in our lives. I see them much the same as he did; yet I would add the phrase *repeatable patterns*. Louie Giglio has a video on YouTube that describes the cell adhesion/protein molecule in the human body called laminin. It is the molecule that holds the body together. Astonishingly, it is shaped like a cross. I am in awe of that being that Colossians 1:17 says He is before all things and by Him all things consist, kind of like the glue that holds everything together. (YouTube it.) Now I'm not a biologist and didn't research this thoroughly, but the little research I have done was consistent with what he had to say regarding laminin. When viewing the earth on Google Earth looking at the rivers and tributaries, you can see certain patterns, much like the types of patterns you see when looking at the veins in someone's arm. There are subtle similar physical features and traits that are passed down genetically from generation to generation. The configuration of our solar system is accurately pictured in the makeup of one of the smallest building blocks of all matter, the atom; electrons in orbit around the centrally located nucleus. The moon, one of the two brightest objects the naked eye can view from earth, appears to shine bright on certain cloudless nights, but it only receives its ability to shine by absorbing energy from the sun. To me, that effectively illustrates the devil (a created being) absorbing his energy from God, so much so that the Bible says that Satan can be transformed into an angel of light, thereby effectively deceiving many.

> And God made two great lights; the greater light to rule
> the day, and the lesser light to rule the night: he made the
> stars also. (Genesis 1:16 KJV)

These are all things that picture (to me) the evidence of a greater design—small patterns that all point to the bigger picture all being held together by the same person, God in the person of Jesus Christ.

In the latter part of Mark 5:7, the demon responded to Christ, "I adjure thee by God, that thou torment me not." The definition of adjure, according to an online dictionary, is, "To charge, bind or command earnestly and solemnly, often under oath or the threat of a penalty." (www.dictionary.com) How could a demon, who is evil, adjure the son of God by God unless there was some precedent set in place by God regarding such matters? The devil, for reasons that God sees fit, has been granted God's permission and the God-given strength, knowledge, ability, and authority to alter God's own creation in Certain numerous ways.

> And the devil said unto him, all this power will I give
> thee, and the glory of them: *for that is delivered unto me;*
> *and to whomsoever I will I give it.* (Luke 4:6 KJV)

Sometimes, truth is stranger than fiction. Why God allows the devil to continue to murder, deceive, and destroy people's lives on this earth is beyond my understanding, except to say that God is a God of His word. He has had many conversations with the devil from the present back to long before we were created. It may be that the Lord is honoring His word, spoken in times past to Lucifer, when he was a covering cherub in the heavenly realm prior to the creation of humankind. God will never violate His word. The following two scriptures are referenced only to show God's relative perspective on His name (Jesus), and the magnitude of esteem He places on His word.

> Wherefore God also hath highly exalted him, and given
> him a name *which is above every name*. (Philippians
> 2:9 KJV)

> For thou hast magnified *thy word above all thy name*.
> (Psalm 138:2 KJV)

It may be that, in contrast, because God is a God of love, He wants His creation, in response to His expressed love in that creation, to serve and worship Him out of a pure heart of genuine love in return being thankful for His provisions regardless of the havoc on earth caused by evil; I believe that is why He gave us and the heavenly hosts a will. He didn't create us as puppets. He's not a dictator. He doesn't fall apart when someone is lifted in pride and disagrees with Him or decides to go in a different direction. He doesn't crumble when we fail Him. As I've heard it put before, "Has it ever occurred to you that nothing has ever occurred to God?" He is God, the one and only true God in existence in heaven and earth. There is none like Him. He is sovereign, meaning there is nothing out of His reach or control. God, Father, Son, and Holy Spirit, planned the death, burial, and resurrection of the Lord Jesus Christ before the world was created. He told the prophets of old of the coming Messiah. In God's timing, He orchestrated all the events leading up to and including this main crescendo event. Prior to His death, burial, and resurrection, Jesus was transfigured in the presence of two witnesses from the Old Testament, Moses (this explains why the Michael and devil were contending for the body of Moses) and Elijah, and three witnesses from the New Testament, Peter, James, and John. That, coupled with the voice of God the Father from within the cloud stating, "This is My beloved Son in Whom I am well pleased," confirms the deity of Jesus Christ as God the Son.

> And after six days Jesus taketh Peter, James, and John his
> brother, and bringeth them up into an high mountain
> apart,

> And was transfigured before them: and his face did shine
> as the sun, and his raiment was white as the light. And,

behold, there appeared unto them Moses and Elias talking with him.

Then answered Peter, and said unto Jesus, Lord, it is good for us to be here: if thou wilt, let us make here three tabernacles; one for thee, and one for Moses, and one for Elias. While he yet spake, behold, a bright cloud overshadowed them: and behold a voice out of the cloud, which said, This is my beloved Son, in whom I am well pleased; hear ye him.

And when the disciples heard it, they fell on their face, and were sore afraid.

And Jesus came and touched them, and said, Arise, and be not afraid. (Mathew 17:1-7 KJV)

Being the only sovereign God in existence throughout all of creation, He has that kind of power and control at His discretion and yet compassionately gives us the truth and allows us to decide for ourselves. In my finite understanding, it seems He allows all to go their own way, knowing that eventually they will come to the end of themselves, be confronted with the truth, and either accept His providential gift of salvation and live intimately in an eternal relationship with Him or refuse His provision and die without Him. The thief on one side of Jesus accepted Christ as Savior, the one on the other side rejected Him as Savior. It was a picture or a parable of all of humankind hanging in the balance between heaven and earth. There is no in between; that is God's place. Jesus is God's sacrificial Lamb, of which there is no greater in heaven and earth. There is only one way to heaven, and we had nothing to do with it; we can only respond to it, in acceptance or rejection. When He said, "It is finished," Satan was defeated, and so was the sting of death.

So when this corruptible shall have put on incorruption, and this mortal shall have put on immortality, then shall be brought to pass the saying that is written, Death is

swallowed up in victory. O death, where is thy sting? O
grave, where is thy victory? (1 Corinthians 15:54–55 KJV)

I find it interesting that God reached down from above, representing
a vertical relationship. Christ reached out to those around Him,
representing a horizontal relationship. When you put the two together,
they form the cross that intersects very near the heart of God. He wants
us to trust in His provision for our sins, for it cost Him the very best that
He had in that He gave His all.

Jesus saith unto him, I am the way, the truth, and the
life: no man cometh unto the Father, but by me. (John
14:6 KJV)

Neither is there salvation in any other: for there is none
other name under heaven given among men, whereby
we must be saved. (Acts 4:12 KJV)

Anyone seriously considering such a life-changing decision needs time
to reason within him or herself and ponder the far-reaching implications
innately included in such a transformation. God, being omniscient and
omnipresent, never disengages from us during that process but allows
us the time to reason and process truth much like the father who closely
monitors the actions of the toddler after telling him or her that the stove
is hot, ever ready to actively intervene on our behalf. So long as we have
breath, we are still able to make that decision to trust Him for salvation.
God provided salvation all by Himself, without our help. It is His gift to
us, if we choose to accept it. If one chooses to reject God's salvation in
a prideful attempt to provide his or her own, it will never meet God's
requirement of righteousness and therefore will be rejected. (This is
vividly pictured in the Old Testament account of God's rejection of Cain's
offering of "the fruit of the ground.") Those individuals who reject God's
salvation will be condemned to eternal separation from God in a hell that
was prepared by God for the devil and his demons. The Bible (the book
of truth) consistently describes hell as a furnace of fire in outer darkness
where there will be weeping and gnashing of teeth for eternity. I find

nothing positive in that statement. Even thinking conservatively on the premise that it's possible that God doesn't exist, one would still have to reason within oneself considering the final outcomes of both scenarios. In one thought, hypothetically, if there is no God, and therefore His rules don't exist, neither are there consequences to our actions, one could live any way one wants according to what seems right in one's own mind at any time one consults it, as it is ever changing. Some "Christians" would have lived a morally acceptable life, seeming to deny themselves of some of the liberties that others enjoy daily. We all die. The result is no real losses, only varying degrees of accomplishment, knowledge, and emotional experience. On the other hand, if God does exist and therefore all His rules and laws exist, one can still live any way one wants, still enjoying oneself daily, not withholding anything from the vivacious heart. Many of those Christians, from the worlds perspective, still seem to live morally correct, often risking their lives in Jesus's name, always trying to push their religion onto others and telling them about Jesus. They work ridiculously hard to try to convert others to their belief system. We all still die in the flesh.

> And as it is appointed unto men once to die, but after this
> the judgment. (Hebrews 9:27 KJV)

Choosing to not believe in the uncompromising laws of electricity, and/or the uncompromising laws of the Lord God Almighty, will not change the reality of violating those laws. The only thing that will change is a person's destiny here on earth and in the life to come. God's word and will still live on accordingly and sometimes with raw efficiency. A person can only choose to accept or reject His provision for his or her life. We only have until we take our last breath or our heart beats its last beat to make this decision. I have seen many people leave this world unexpectedly in what appears to be a premature death.

> That if thou shalt confess with thy mouth the Lord Jesus,
> and shalt believe in thine heart that God hath raised him
> from the dead, thou shalt be saved. For with the heart
> man believeth unto righteousness; and with the mouth

confession is made unto salvation. For the scripture saith, Whosoever believeth on him shall not be ashamed. (Romans 10:9–11 KJV)

For whosoever shall call upon the name of the Lord shall be saved. (Romans 10:13 KJV)

For the wages of sin is death; but the gift of God is eternal life through Jesus Christ our Lord. (Romans 6:23 KJV)

All that the Father giveth me shall come to me; and him that cometh to me I will in no wise cast out. For I came down from heaven, not to do mine own will, but the will of him that sent me. And this is the Father's will which hath sent me, that of all which he hath given me I should lose nothing, but should raise it up again at the last day. (John 6:37–39 KJV)

Behold therefore the goodness and severity of God: on them which fell, severity; but toward thee, goodness, if thou continue in his goodness: otherwise thou also shalt be cut off. (Romans 11:22 KJV)

For we shall all stand before the judgment seat of Christ. (Romans 14:10 KJV; only for believers)

As I understand it from scripture, all true believers in Christ will stand before the judgment seat of Christ and give an account of their lives and their words as to what they did with the salvation He gave them. If they sought to live life in the flesh, glory, riches, and possessions, they will suffer loss, but their souls will be saved, and they will receive rewards for what was done for Christ and the advancement of His kingdom. If they devoted their lives to dying daily to self, allowing the Holy Spirit of God to rule in their hearts and minds ordering their very steps, they will receive great rewards in the kingdom of heaven and will be given rule over many. I'm not entirely sure of the scope of what this statement encompasses, but it seems to carry a significant amount of gravity with it.

> For other foundation can no man lay than that is laid, which is Jesus Christ. Now if any man build upon this foundation gold, silver, precious stones, wood, hay, stubble; Every man's work shall be made manifest: for the day shall declare it, because it shall be revealed by fire; and the fire shall try every man's work of what sort it is. If any man's work abide which he hath built thereupon, he shall receive a reward. If any man's work shall be burned, he shall suffer loss: but he himself shall be saved; yet so as by fire. (1 Corinthians 3:11–15 KJV)

> For we must all appear before the judgment seat of Christ; that every one may receive the things done in his body, according to that he hath done, whether it be good or bad. (2 Corinthians 5:10 KJV)

Regarding heaven, Jesus says there are many mansions that He has gone to prepare for us, and I believe (I use a lot of imagination here, but according to His word, He is intimately connected with us and knows the desires of our hearts) they will be tailored to each individual preference accordingly, to his or her personal interests and passions. I would imagine that these mansions would be filled with the things that you are personally passionate about, whether they be horses, cats, bowling alleys, muscle cars, paintings, football or origami, music, science, the medical field, astronomy, motorcycles, bicycles, you name it (or at least in the spirit of such things)—things that would truly mean something *to you,* even if no one else on the planet knows about it, of course only in accordance with His will. If you enjoy preparing meals, I would imagine yours might contain the most elaborate kitchen with double ovens, a huge stainless-steel refrigerator, a preparation island with sinks, a garbage disposal, and hopefully a dishwasher, but it will all be there for you, having come from the desires of your own heart. If you enjoy hunting, I imagine there being a vast array of things related to hunting, as the fullness of God is adequately displayed in the earth and all that it contains. The fact that He did all of this in seven days is amazingly impressive; imagine all He could do since then on our behalf, knowing our every thought, and that it is His delight as a heavenly Father to bring joy to His children. I remember my cousin and I conversing about pets from our childhood perhaps being in heaven. My contention was that I haven't read anything to support that theory. After pondering this topic, I believe I was wrong. I truly believe that God knows our intimate desires and has thought of everything to smallest detail. Just look at the nature that surrounds you. I have no proof of this except to say that it seems to be consistent with His nature and His word. You could probably walk outside, step off the front porch, and look under a rock or board that's been there for any lengthy amount of time and just be amazed at all the life working together under there or take a walk into the woods nearby and just look around at all the amazing detail that surrounds you and then close your eyes and listen to the wonder that surrounds you in all its beauty.

The Great White Throne Judgment
(Only for Nonbelievers)

> And I saw a great white throne, and him that sat on it, from whose face the earth and the heaven fled away; and there was found no place for them. And I saw the dead, small and great, stand before God; and the books were opened: and another book was opened, which is the book of life: and the dead were judged out of those things which were written in the books, according to their works. And the sea gave up the dead which were in it; and death and hell delivered up the dead which were in them: and they were judged every man according to their works. And death and hell were cast into the lake of fire. This is the second death. And whosoever was not found written in the book of life was cast into the lake of fire. (Revelations 20:11–15 KJV)

THOSE WHO HAVE REJECTED JESUS Christ's provision for sin will be held accountable for their own sin ("for the wages of sin is death") at the great white throne judgment, and since there is nothing in and of man's effort that God the Father would consider an acceptable payment, it will be rejected. It's not negotiable.

Old Testament

I have sworn by myself, the word is gone out of my mouth in righteousness, and shall not return, That unto me every knee shall bow, every tongue shall swear. (Isaiah 45:23 KJV)

New Testament

As I live, saith the Lord, every knee shall bow to me, and every tongue shall confess to God. So then every one of us shall give account of himself to God. (Romans 14:11–12 KJV)

The fact of the matter is that *all* will bow down before the throne of God and pay homage to the Father, Son, and Holy Ghost. True believers will then spend eternity enjoying (coupled with fear I'm sure) an intimate relationship with an understanding God who calls them friends. Unbelievers will spend eternity separated from God in a lake of fire where there will be tormented, with weeping and gnashing of teeth. The point I was endeavoring to make is that thinking conservatively would be the only logical choice. There are no magical phrases that will get you there. There is no such thing as luck. Eating Lucky Charms won't do it. Wearing lucky charms won't do it. Much like President Abraham Lincoln's response to a verbal debate that ended in principal disagreement, while it is certain that both parties could be, and one must be, wrong, it is not possible for both to be right. Knowing that there is a significant amount of suffering involved with being a Christian, considering the alternative and the end thereof, the option of trusting Christ as Savior and His finished work on the cross is far less dreadful; although the eighteen-inch tragedy is undoubtedly one of the saddest, that's the approximate distance from your head to your heart. You can have head knowledge of the Lord Jesus Christ and His death, burial, and resurrection just as the devil does and still not believe in Him from the heart unto salvation. Recognizing that He is, always has been, and always will be God is a great place to start because it removes all possibilities of false doctrine brought on by the slight of men as Jesus conducted Himself only as the Father directed Him, even to the denying of the flesh and willfully submitting Himself to His impending death on the cross, knowing that, as God, at any time He could have stopped the whole thing, calling on myriads of angels.

All of God's attributes are absolute. They are directly related to those uncompromising universal laws. He is unchanging. He is always faithful. What He says, He will do. He does have a plan for His creation, again collective as well as individual. I've been told that no two snowflakes are the same, and while I'm glad I didn't have to do that study, I find it remarkable that in God's vast array of creation of variety, individuality still seems to be important to Him. Likewise, we were uniquely created by intelligent design, with individual personalities, in His image. He is a triune being, Father (soul), Son (body), and Spirit. He created us after the same triune image, body, soul, and spirit. He is an eternal being; likewise, since conception, we also will exist for eternity. Life may appear to end on this earth when death comes to the flesh, but the soul (the mind, will, and emotions) and the spirit will live on forever; and according to the Bible, the flesh will be changed.

> Behold, I shew you a mystery; We shall not all sleep, but we shall all be changed, In a moment, in the twinkling of an eye, at the last trump: for the trumpet shall sound, and the dead shall be raised incorruptible, and we shall be changed. (1 Corinthians 15:51–52 KJV)

I realize it seems to go against our understanding when we lose loved ones. A torrent of emotion seems to consume our entire being, leaving its mark while slowly losing energy, leaving sadness, loneliness, a sense of emptiness, and oftentimes even anger in its wake. Our feelings do not change the truth of God's word. We all have lost loved ones in life who we were so very close to, and being faced with the knowledge contained in the word of God regarding our finite fleshly existence, we are sure to be concerned with our own eternal status at some point. Might I just say that the Holy Spirit of God has endeavored to reach all of humankind with the same heartfelt compassion in sincerity.

There was a certain rich man, which was clothed in purple and fine linen, fared sumptuously every day: And there was a certain beggar named Lazarus which was laid at his gate, full of sores, and desiring to be fed with the crumbs that fell from the rich man's table: moreover the dogs came and licked his sores. And it came to pass, that the beggar died, and that he was carried away by the angels into Abraham's bosom: the rich man died also, and was buried; And in hell he lift up his eyes, being in torments, and seeth Abraham afar off, and Lazarus in his bosom. And he cried and said, Father Abraham, have mercy on me, and send Lazarus, that he may dip the tip of his finger in water, and cool my tongue; for I am tormented in this flame. But Abraham said, Son, remember that thou in thy lifetime receivedst thy good things, and likewise Lazarus evil things: but now he is comforted and thou art tormented. And besides all this, between us and you there is a great gulf fixed: so that they which would pass from hence to you cannot; neither can they pass to us, that would come from thence. Then he said, I pray thee therefore, father, that thou wouldest send him to my father's house: For I have five brethren; that he may testify unto them, lest they also come to this place of torment. Abraham saith unto him, They have Moses and the prophets; let them hear them. And he said, Nay, father Abraham: but if one went unto them from the dead, they will repent. And he said unto him, If they hear not Moses and the prophets, neither will they be persuaded, though one rose from the dead. (Luke 16:19–31 KJV)

Just as sure as there will be many in heaven who are surprised to be there, the Lord warns that there will be some in hell pleading with Him, saying, "Lord, Lord, did I not do things in Your name?"

He will reply, "Depart from me. I never knew you."

God cannot be outwitted. Beware of that false sense of security.

Don't outsmart yourself. While God does have many mysteries on this planet, many things He has made very simple, clear, and straightforward, including His plan of salvation. What could be clearer than "we are sinners"? What could be simpler than to "believe on Him unto salvation"? I'm reminded of the story of the man who ignored the obvious events that preceded his death.

> A man sitting in his home watching the TV newscast was made aware that there was a flood headed his way, to which he said in his heart, "God will save me." He later heard on the radio that the authorities were evacuating the city, to which he replied under his breath, "God will take care of me." The waters began rising and the police knocked on his door, warning him of the impending danger, to which he replied, "God takes care of me." On the second floor of his home at the window, he turned away a canoe, repeating that God was his savior. The last event preceding his death was him refusing help from folks in a helicopter because he was waiting on God's provision to save him. In heaven with tears in his eyes, he requested of the Lord, "Lord, I trusted you. Why did you not save me?" The Lord replied, "My son, I sent you a newscaster on TV, a radio broadcast, policemen to your door step, a canoe to your second-story window, and a helicopter to your roof. What more did you want me to do?" (Origin unknown)

If you are reading this, it is no accident. While it's true of heaven that you can't get there from here on your own efforts, God in His infinite wisdom has already factored that into the equation and made the only adequate provision possible on our behalf. If you've read this far, perhaps this has found its way into your hands through God's complex network of choreography. Perhaps He is endeavoring to reason with you on a personal level. Maybe you just read this because you were curious or were humoring the author. Please, don't ignore the truth. Everyone has doubts, unanswered questions, heartaches, and perplexities in life, but don't let them deter you from responding to the truth. If you, even in its smallest measurement, are curious or heard the still, small voice of God in your heart regarding the content of this book, then at least voice your questions and concerns (in private) to God in all sincerity. Challenge Him to prove Himself to you beyond the shadow of a doubt. God is an understanding God. He is a just God. As the only truth, He cannot deny Himself, and He cannot lie. While there may be many truths, truth in and of itself is singular. Truth is self-existent, self-sustaining, uncompromising, and unbiased. This is not where it ends. Life in this world is a temporary assignment at best. As perplexing as this life is at times, it is even more confusing to me to think of what comes in the next, although I rest in understanding the knowledge that God knows.

> Let us hear the conclusion of the whole matter: Fear God, and keep His commandments: for this is the whole duty of man. (Ecclesiastes 12:13 KJV)

> But ye shall receive power, after that the Holy Ghost is come upon you: and ye shall be witnesses unto me both in Jerusalem, and in all Judaea, and in Samaria, and unto the uttermost part of the earth. (Acts 1:8 KJV)

About the Author

Sean is a family man who works as a welding inspector by trade. Answering the perceived need to write, he endeavors to share with the reader some of life's most important principals regarding the non-negotiable circumstances included in the finiteness of life in the light of eternal, universal truths found in the word of God. Additionally, he shares in this journey some of his personal experiences in recognizing some of these life changing principals and the profound impact they have had on him and his family.

Special thanks to those that inspire the author:

The Lord Jesus Christ
My wife and Children
Pastor William J. Moore
Pastor Richard Skiver
Pastor Phil Hillditch
Pastor Tony Evans
Pastor Charles Stanley
Pastor Alistair Begg
Pastor John Macarthur
Pastor Mike Lavelle

Pastor Joe McCray
Pastor Richard Barth
Elizabeth Elliot
Brad Young
Brian Reese
Brian Smith
Charles Spurgeon
George Mueller
James Elliot

Printed in the United States
By Bookmasters